# I can add up

## Ray Gibson

### Illustrated by Amanda Barlow
### Edited by Fiona Watt

Series editor : Jenny Tyler

# Contents

| | | | |
|---|---|---|---|
| Starting out | 2 | Spotty animal | 18 |
| Funny clowns | 4 | Snowman | 20 |
| Mice and cheese | 6 | In the garden | 22 |
| Pretty princesses | 8 | Penguin party | 24 |
| Bears and bees | 10 | Hungry turtles | 26 |
| Caterpillar's shoes | 12 | Wheels on the train | 28 |
| A castle and flags | 14 | Jolly juggler | 30 |
| Teeth and tentacles | 16 | Sheep in a field | 32 |

With thanks to Gillian Thumpston

# Starting out

This book is full of activities which ask you to cut things out or find things and add them to the pictures. Sometimes, you will have to take some of the things away and count again. Cut the things out quickly and don't worry about how neat they are.

When you start to add up, point to each thing as you count it and say the number. Later, when you are good at adding up, you may not need to point to things as you count.

You may find it easiest to start counting from the left side of a page and move to the right.

How many butterflies have spots?
Cut some spots for the others. Put them on.
How many butterflies have spots now?

3

# Funny clowns

How many clowns
have hats?
Cut out hats for
the other clowns.
How many hats
are there now?

How many blocks have
spots?
Cut spots for the rest.
How many spots are
there now?

# Mice and cheese

How many mice have tails?
How many mice have no tails?

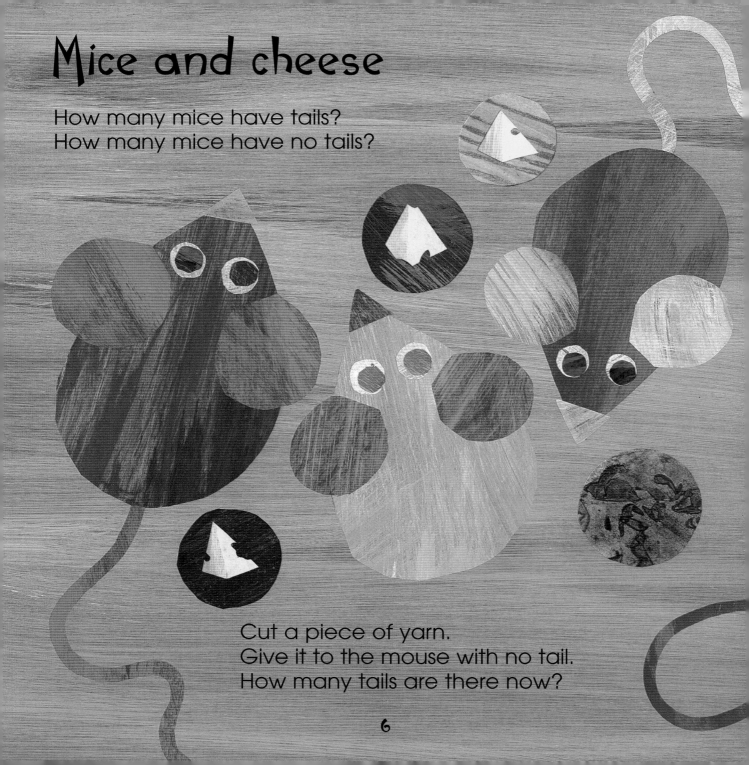

Cut a piece of yarn.
Give it to the mouse with no tail.
How many tails are there now?

6

How many plates have cheese?
How many empty plates are there?

Cut some yellow paper.
Put a piece on each empty plate.
How many pieces of cheese are there now?

# Pretty princesses

How many princesses have crowns?
Cut out a paper crown. Give it to the princess without one.
How many crowns are there now?

How many rings have jewels? Cut out jewels for the rest.
How many jewels are there now?

# Bears and bees

How many bears are awake?
Draw and cut out open eyes
for the others.
Put them on the sleeping
bears.
How many are
awake now?

2 honey pots have lids.
Cut out lids for the others.
How many lids are there now?

Count the bees on the
other page.
Add on the bees on this page.
How many bees altogether?

# Caterpillar's shoes

Count the butterflies on this page.
Add on the ones on the other page.
How many altogether?

4 flowers have leaves.
Cut a leaf for the
other flower.
How many now?

How many shoes is the
caterpillar wearing?
How many legs have
no shoes?

Cut shoes from paper
and put them on his
legs.
How many shoes are
there now?

# A castle and flags

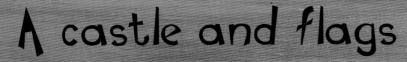

How many windows
are on the castle?
Cut **3** more from
paper and put them
on the castle.
How many windows
are there now?

How many flagpoles
have flags?
Cut out **2** more and
put them on empty
flagpoles.
How many flags are
there now?

How many rocks?
Add **1** more.
How many rocks
are there now?

# Teeth and tentacles

How many teeth does the big fish have?
Give him 3 paper teeth.
How many teeth are
there now?

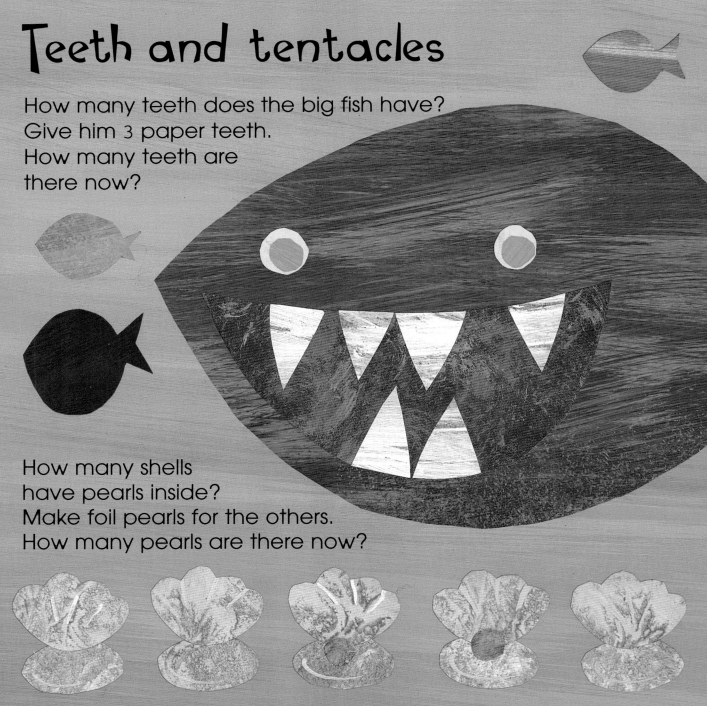

How many shells
have pearls inside?
Make foil pearls for the others.
How many pearls are there now?

How many tentacles
does the octopus have?
Cut **2** more from yarn.
How many now?

# Spotty animal

How many nests
have eggs?
Cut out **3** more eggs.
How many eggs are
there now?

How many spots does
this animal have?
Cut out **5** more spots.
Put them on the
animal.
How many spots
are there now?

19

# Snowman

How many buttons does the
snowman have?
Cut **4** more from paper.
Put them on his tummy.
How many are there now?

How many birds
have a tail?
Cut paper tails for
the others.
How many tails are
there now?

Cut out **1** snowflake
from paper.
Add it to the others.
How many are there
altogether?

21

# In the garden

How many flowers are on the bush?
Cut out **3** more flowers and
add them.
How many are there now?
Caterpillars eat **2** of the
flowers. Take them off.
How many flowers are left?

How many pots have a worm on top?
Cut more worms from yarn for the others.
How many worms are there now?

How many carrots
have leaves?
Cut out a paper leaf
for the one without.
How many carrots
have leaves now?

# Penguin party

How many penguins have fish?
Cut out **6** more and give them to the penguins.
How many fish are there now?

Three penguins ate their fish.
Take **3** fish away.
How many fish are there now?

How many icebergs are in the sea?
Add **2** more.
How many are there now?

# Hungry turtles

How many turtles have a leaf to eat?
Cut out leaves and give them to the others.
How many turtles are eating now?

**1** turtle finishes his
leaf.
Take **1** leaf away.
How many leaves
are left?

# Wheels on the train

How many wheels does the train have?
Add buttons for the missing wheels.
How many wheels are there altogether?

How many parcels are in the wagons?
Add 3 more. How many now?
One parcel falls out. Take 1 away. How many are there now?

# Jolly juggler

How many shapes
are balancing below?
Cut out **4** more and
put them on top.
How many are
there now?
**3** shapes topple off.
Take **3** away.
How many are left?

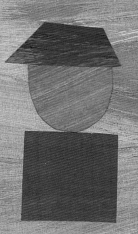

Count the red
clubs. How many
are there?
Count the blue
ones. How many
altogether?

This juggler is juggling 3 things. Cut 3 more things from a magazine and put them on. How many is he juggling now?

The juggler drops 2 things. Take 2 of them away. How many things are there now?

31

# Sheep in a field

How many sheep are in the field?
How many more do you
need to make 10?
Use your fingers to
help you count.

How many more
flowers do you need
to make 10?
How many more
birds will make 10?